Montauk is

W. D. Akin

New York, NY
Sag Harbor, NY

Harbor Electronic Publishing 2005
www.HEPDigital.com

Copyright © 2005 W. D. Akin

No part of this publication may be reproduced, stored in a retrieval system, or transmitted, in any form or by any means without the prior permission of Harbor Electronic Publishing. Permission is granted to photocopy any part of the book under contract with the Copyright Clearance Center (www.copyright.com).

Library of Congress Catalogue Card Number:
2005923826
ISBN (paper): 1-932916-03-2
First Printing May 2005
Printed in the United States of America

CREDITS:
All Photos by W. D. Akin
Editor: Charles Monaco
Cover Design: Joseph Dunn

A NOTE ON THE TYPE:
This book is set in Baskerville. The font bears the name of John Baskerville, an English printer and typographer who developed the typeface in the eighteenth century. Baskerville was a life-long friend of Benjamin Franklin, who used the typeface in his print shop. The font's clear, sharp image set it apart from other fonts of its time.

Montauk is

W. D. Akin

Acknowledgment

I would like to thank Brandon Ayre who saw this collection first and without hesitating urged me to keep going. Also Celine Keating and Laura Stein for their constructive comments and encouragement, Richard Kahn for several critical editorial suggestions, and Jill Flemming for her last minute observations. I would also like to thank the Reverend Howard Friend for decades of inspiration. Finally, my wife Monika; she has never hedged her opinion, in this instance positive, and I doubt she ever will.

W. D. Akin

If you can't discover the Truth where you are, where do you think you will find it?

—Buddhist Text

In the end, our society will be defined not by what it creates, but by what it refuses to destroy.

—John Sawhill (1936–2000)

The sound of water says what I think.

—Chuang Tzu (370–301 B.C.)

Table of Contents

Introduction. 9

Haiku is. 11

Montauk is 13

Introduction

I first came to Montauk in 1950. My father had run his wooden speedboat out from our summer home in Westhampton, and mother and I drove out to meet him at the Montauk Yacht Club. That afternoon he took us for a ride out past the lighthouse into the Atlantic Ocean and then west along the cliffs on the south side. I recall how disappointed I was that I could still see land, how could this be the ocean?

Over the next half century I was never away from Montauk for more than a few winter months, and two years in the Navy. As a boy I spent hundreds of hours fishing in the local lakes, from the docks at night, and along the shore. Almost always alone. I hunted (unsuccessfully) over the windswept grassy hills with my bow and arrow for quail, pheasant, and deer. I learned to surf when the waves were combed back by a fresh northwest breeze or when glassy calm emerging out of a thick fog. I dug clams and dove for bay scallops in Lake Montauk. Fishing offshore with my father and others I learned about the big fish—swordfish, giant tuna, marlin—and also how beautiful, lonely, dangerous and unforgiving the ocean can be.

Montauk is

All these activities were enjoyed thoroughly by the child and the young man who followed. But looking back it is clear that other forces were at work, influences that would over time bring me greater satisfaction than the fun and games I was consumed with through those early decades.

Today I recognize how much more there is to Montauk. Even the winds have personality and rhythm. The southeast wind roars off the ocean beating rain against windows. The bone-dry northwest wind moves the sand, and brushes back the cresting ocean waves. In summer the southwest wind spreads the salt spray across the land, and inhales the honeysuckle perfume from the brush. Continuing across this tiny peninsula, it lifts aromas off the water and boats in Montauk harbor, and with one last surge swirls through crowds of summer visitors searching the inlet shops for some treasure to carry home as a reminder of this magical place. Finally there is the northeast winter wind, the Snowman. This force, carved into the history of the New England coast, carries no mercy for shorelines, houses, or those sheltered within. All together these winds live forever in the present moment, inviting those who dare to join them.

Montauk is touches on many of the aspects I have come to love most about this place. I hope those who know the land and water, and perhaps even visitors who have had just a small taste, will be able to identify with the experiences as expressed in these few words. And while each individual must discover a resonance with Montauk in his or her own way, the source remains the same.

Haiku is

Originating in seventeenth century Japan, *haiku* in its most pure form is a seventeen-syllable poem expressed on three lines of five, seven, and five syllables. However, even those poets writing in Japanese have from the very beginning violated this strict rule. A more useful definition, especially outside the confines of the original Japanese, is to view the poems as expressions that attempt to capture 'a moment in time' by juxtaposing two often dissimilar perspectives or ideas, thus jolting the reader's sense of expectation. This is not unlike aspects of Zen Buddhism such as the *koan*, or mind puzzle.

In this collection I have taken more liberty with the form than even contemporary authorities might be willing to accept. I reserve my apologies, however, for the true haiku masters, including Basho (1644–1694), Buson (1715–1783), Issa (1763–1783), and many others.

W. D. Akin
Montauk
March 2005

In Montauk,
so lucky to be served first.
Fresh sunrise.

Montauk is

The jetty horn
again and again this morning.
A soothing sound
here on land.

Montauk is
___

Arriving at the beach
I am a child again.
Thank God for dirt roads.

Montauk is:
T-shirt.
No shirt.
Sweat shirt.
Nightshirt.

Montauk is

On my bike to the lighthouse
the smell of wild grapes:
school has started.

Giant waves carve away rocky cliffs.
Howling winds scream through fishing boat masts.
An occasional reminder
about who's in charge.

Montauk is

White, red, speckled, brown,
round, smooth, flat, big, and small rocks.
Which one,
or two,
to carry home?

Montauk is

Six degrees of separation,
but ten degrees of local.
Welcome to Montauk.

Montauk is:
waves from Bermuda
rocks from Canada,
and a surfer from Babylon.

Sparkling sand surrounds my feet,
 and then at night
above me in the sky.

M o n t a u k   i s

After
the bus
or car,
or train,
that first breath.

Montauk is

March ends
with three warm days,
then at night, joyful voices:
peepers.

M o n t a u k   i s

The jetties are frozen over:
in my truck
the coffee tastes even better.

Friends arrive
and then depart.
Once more I am alone
with the wind.

Montauk is

On me so soon
this December darkness.
Will the sun come back next year?

West on 27
up the first hill
and a glimpse of ocean in the mirror.
Can I turn back?

M o n t a u k   i s

Swordfish and marlin,
scallops from the lake:
soon gone,
almost forgotten.

Montauk is

A cold northwest wind,
and from the bluff
surfers watch anxiously:
overnight the storm swells arrived.

Montauk is
morning dew on my car.
It will blow from the Southwest today.

Montauk is

Memorial Day,
and people,
and cars,
and something moving in the bushes:
this year's fawn.

M o n t a u k   i s

A path through the dunes,
warm sand,
hot sand,
fried feet.
To the water,
run!

Montauk is

Kids and kites,
towels and tans,
balls and boards,
skin and sand.
August before September.

Summer party invitations,
well intended celebrations.
Like to go,
but want to stay,
home
just once,
tonight,
please.

Montauk is

Montauk is
a commercial fisherman
with a six handicap.

East wind,
driving rain,
diving birds:
rubber men are waving plastic poles.

M o n t a u k   i s

Pounding surf,
moving dunes,
high tide,
low tide:
so much peace.

So many waves.
One after another,
just like people,
none the same.

M o n t a u k   i s

Soft rocks,
hard water.
Or so it seems
as years pass.

M o n t a u k   i s
―――――――――――

This clear September morning
the wind is northwest.
Connecticut floats above the water.

Montauk is

Wet, warm, cold, hard,
dry, soft, steady, gentle,
pleasant, penetrating,
annoying, feared,
unwanted, welcomed,
praised and biting
      wind.

Big boats charge out to sea.
Standing in the surf
I cast my line.

Montauk is
———————————

A great fish.
the biggest in the whole ocean!
I had him on,
Really dad!

Fly fishing from the inlet shallows,
the restaurant crowd is watching.
Please, Neptune,
a big one.

Be
as if you walk in shallow water:
footsteps firm
that leave no trace.

Montauk is

Montauk is
hard rocks,
rough seas,
a calm heart.

On this foggy beach
the wind is as wet as the ocean.
No need for a swim.

Montauk is

The orchestral leaves have fallen,
now I hear only the skeleton keys:
December wind.

Montauk is

Montauk is
a storm wind
that sings with the sea,
blows chords through the trees,
and beats rhythm into the soul.

Montauk is

A mile from the ocean
I hear the waves.
Why can't I hear the stars?

This glorious first day of autumn
falls victim to my thoughts:
soon December.

Montauk is

Walking
in the fog,
A glimpse of what my mirror cannot show.

Another shooting star,
and again the same wish.
Only time will tell.

M o n t a u k   i s

Never have met
a dishonest dog.
Makes me wish
we all had tails.

"I was here when…"
"It's a dry summer…"
"This year for sure…"
"We're way overdue…"
The Big One haunts us.

Montauk is
___

Casting again and again,
but no fish bites.
So?

One small room
with my dog
in February:
a perfect crowd.

Montauk is

No stop lights,
      just one mail box,
and it's at the post office.

Montauk is

Words,
like breaking waves,
my soaring thoughts
crash on the page.

Montauk is

Along the beach
fishnets, buoys, and bottles:
all plastic.
Progress floats upon the ocean.

Montauk is

The jetty horn is a G#:
music everywhere.

Montauk:
no good weather,
no bad weather,
just strong character.

M o n t a u k   i s

The penetrating lighthouse beacon,
the "hooter" foghorn,
and the ten second radar beep.
They were forever,
or so it seemed.

Thunder and lightning in the dark,
with dawn a northwest wind.
My musty closet can breathe again.

Montauk is

Seagulls are gathering
on the fairways and in the hollows.
Such good weathermen.

Digging a new garden,
more stones than dirt:
an abundant harvest of Montauk potatoes.

Montauk is

Long ago they came to this beach;
quartz, feldspar, garnets and schist:
Canadian immigrants.

Montauk is

In Montauk
keep time,
maybe.

M o n t a u k   i s

"Fresh Montauk Swordfish,"
oh how the menus lie.

Watching wave after wave
until
at last
my mind is empty.

Montauk is

Water south,
water east,
water north.
And west
twelve million of the richest people on earth.
Montauk, I pray for your future.

Fishing was better then.
Maybe they are just hiding.

M o n t a u k   i s

June sunsets over Connecticut,
by December over the ocean.
Time flies.

Beach plums, blueberries,
blackberries, and grapes.
But I know where the cranberries are.

Montauk is

Our summer guests left last night.
Today my tour guide cap
is just a hat.

Every Montauk local
is slightly bent…
by the wind.

Montauk is

Alone again in September
with an occasional thought
about those who have returned
to where the news is made.

Montauk is

Problems with love,
problems with money,
and the world news.
How lucky the minnows
with only the birds above and the fish below.

Once again
the crowds have gone,
and taken my loneliness with them.

M o n t a u k   i s

Hemingway, Farrington,
Tommy Gifford,
Buddy Merritt,
Ralph Pitts:
my heros are gone,
and the ocean?
it too seems sad.

Fish traps set along the bay beach
for three hundred years.
And tomorrow?

**Suddenly wealthy beyond my dreams:
gold dust in the sunlight
this autumn afternoon.**

Fishermen
casting at dawn:
are they trying to catch the sun?

Montauk is

Monopoly, Yahtzee,
    Parcheesi, Go Fish.
Rich memories
of rainy days.

Montauk is

Between an endless ocean
and a carved and contoured land,
sanctuary:
this stretch of changing sand.

Montauk is

Every day it changes:
the sand shifts,
rocks are uncovered,
and debris washes up
on this place I call me.

Montauk is

Pulling so many closer and closer
this magnate,
this ocean
that bites.

We cover your surface with debris.
We suffocate your ripples with slicks of oil.
We strip you of your countless living creatures
and suck them into our bellies.
How dare we condemn you when you fight back!

Montauk is

Up on the mast
with only the sky and ocean
wherever I turn:
an infinite blue stage.

M o n t a u k   i s

The old fisherman went to sea,
to see
his old friends,
the fish.

Fish,
I have caught you once,
twice,
and more.
Do I need to catch you again?

M o n t a u k   i s

Rain drops
and sticky grains of sand:
little things have changed my plans.

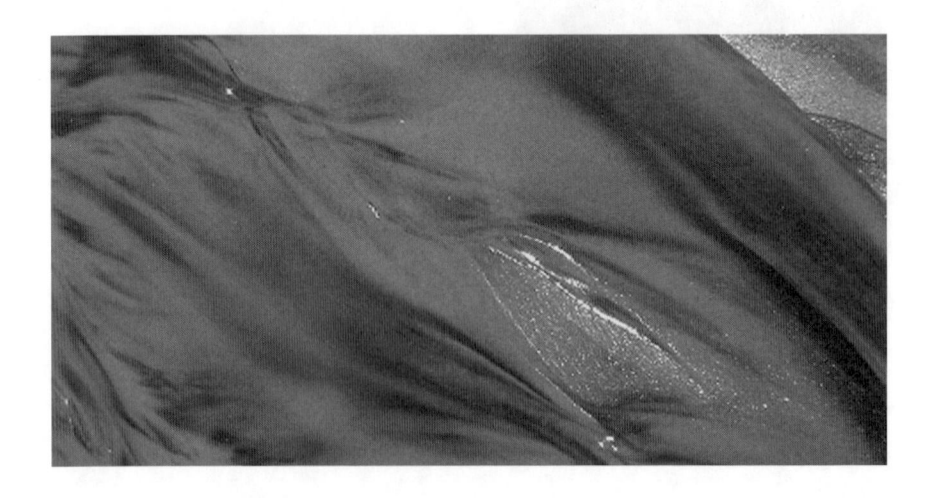

M o n t a u k   i s

Bigger fish equals
bigger man.
God, how did we get here?

Carrying groceries to my car,
    I hear them again over the dunes:
ocean breakers.

Montauk is

The weekend jogger
is passing the songbirds' favorite pond:
too bad about the earphones.

M o n t a u k   i s

Celebrating yesterday and tomorrow
in poetry and song.
A pity today is all about the mortgage.

M o n t a u k   i s
_____

Daylight dissolves into the sea,
now darkness on steroids…
Montauk fog.

Cookies at home, Gaviola's, and the bank!
So lucky to be
a dog in Montauk.

Montauk is

Boats leave and return,
tides flood and ebb,
streams drain and cleanse the land.
Lake Montauk is busy night and day.

Montauk is

I have many friends in Montauk:
some,
a few,
are people.

This sunny day,
these sparkling waves:
so easy to forget
the darkness of the universe.

Montauk is

Who am I?
Why bother to ask,
that person left on the Jitney.

M   o   n   t   a   u   k   i   s

From the fog and wind
the visitors turn away,
as if able to feed only on sunshine.

Salt shaker:
simple
elegant
practical
and useless in July.

Montauk is

This fog
opens to let me pass,
and closes behind.
Door after door.

Alone on the beach,
feeling guilty for so much peace:
glassy calm Gardiners Bay.

M o n t a u k   i s

Montauk is

Sneaking in my office window
the fog horn
shatters my computer screen.

Montauk koan:
Waves in the ocean,
thoughts in the mind,
which holds more?

Once toy shovels and seashells,
today vermouth and gin:
each adult a child in decay.

M o n t a u k   i s

As we keep coming
this land, Montauk,
where can it run?

Montauk is

Big, little, huge, tiny,
jagged, slippery, smooth,
round, red, grey, blond, and freckled:
rock stars.

Overlooked on clear days
suddenly reacquainted this foggy evening.
My two small oak trees.

These wind chimes and the mockingbird:
do they relate so well
when I am away?

Montauk is

One day the sun,
the next a storm:
this ocean bluff is not so foolish
to think there is a choice.

Reach for the sun
pale evergreen buds.
Too soon the snow will fall.

Racing across my driveway
another busy day
for the turtle.

M o n t a u k   i s

Your old wrinkled face
so beautiful:
Shadmoor cliffs.

Montauk is

A thousand times the same scream
as gulls and terns crash the surface,
each one a karate master.

Christmas lights on the gazebo,
and a shamrock,
and Feliz Navidad.
Welcome to Montauk.

M o n t a u k   i s

Crossing the Atlantic
you trip over Montauk:
refreshing east wind.

Between the ocean and the land
at least this inlet
is calm.

Thinking of this,
and that,
and this.
No time to hear the wind.

This house was in the sun,
out of the wind,
near the lake:
smart builders, those Indians.

M o n t a u k   i s
___

Fresh out of the sea
the first bite is so sweet.
Each sunrise.

Outside the inlet fashion shops
white seagulls
and black cormorants fish.

M o n t a u k   i s

It seems so lost
on the beach
this blanket of snow.

M o n t a u k   i s

Montauk is
heavy fog and a gentle breeze:
perfect day for a walk!

M o n t a u k   i s

Europe to New York
twenty minutes before landing:
look,
down there,
out the port windows.

Relief and joy.
Thank you for coming home:
shadbush blossoms.

Montauk winter:
happy to get away,
happy to come home,
happy to repeat.

Montauk is

Millions of years learning to eat,
no wonder they take the bait:
shark fishing.

So friendly and gentle.
What was her name,
that last gust of wind?

Cruel
and unusual
punishment:
April in Montauk.

M o n t a u k   i s

Each wave breaks
      and dissolves back into the sea.
And so it is
with everything.

For Bob

Every year more new surfers,
but forever
your empty wave.

Montauk is

M o n t a u k   i s

Sixty years now,
      so many islands,
one home.